BOOKS BY PHILIP LEVINE

WHAT WORK IS

WHAT WORK IS

POEMS BY

PHILIP LEVINE

ALFRED A. KNOPF   NEW YORK   1991

THIS IS A BORZOI BOOK
PUBLISHED BY ALFRED A. KNOPF, INC.

My thanks to the editors of the following publications in which these poems first appeared:

Antaeus ("Soloing")
The Atlantic Monthly ("Among Children")
The Georgia Review ("Coming Homeward from the Post Office")
The Gettysburg Review ("The Seventh Summer")
Michigan Quarterly Review ("My Grave")
The New England Review ("The Sweetness of Bobby Hefka," "Facts," & "Coming of Age in Michigan")
The New Yorker ("Fear and Fame," "Coming Close," "Fire," "Every Blessed Day," "What Work Is," "Snails," "Perennials," "Above the World," "M. Degas Teaches Art & Science at Durfee Intermediate School," and "On the River")
Poetry ("Burned" and "The Right Cross")
Western Humanities Review ("Growth" and "Scouting")
Zyzzyva ("Gin")

My special thanks to my friends who helped me with these poems and encouraged me to complete them, especially to Larry Levis, Garrett Hongo, Edward Hirsch, Donald Hall, Sharon Olds, and C.K. Williams.

Library of Congress Cataloging-in-Publication Data
Levine, Philip, 1928–
    What work is : poems / Philip Levine.
        p.   cm.
    ISBN 0–679–40166–0
    I.   Title.
PS3562.E9W47   1991
811'.54—dc20   90–53421
                                                                          CIP

Manufactured in the United States of America
Published May 10, 1991
Second Printing, August 1991

FOR LARRY LEVIS

CONTENTS

FEAR AND FAME

Half an hour to dress, wide rubber hip boots,
gauntlets to the elbow, a plastic helmet
like a knight's but with a little glass window
that kept steaming over, and a respirator
to save my smoke-stained lungs. I would descend
step by slow step into the dim world
of the pickling tank and there prepare
the new solutions from the great carboys
of acids lowered to me on ropes—all from a recipe
I shared with nobody and learned from Frank O'Mera
before he went off to the bars on Vernor Highway
to drink himself to death. A gallon of hydrochloric
steaming from the wide glass mouth, a dash
of pale nitric to bubble up, sulphuric to calm,
metals for sweeteners, cleansers for salts,
until I knew the burning stew was done.
Then to climb back, step by stately step, the adventurer
returned to the ordinary blinking lights
of the swingshift at Feinberg and Breslin's
First-Rate Plumbing and Plating with a message
from the kingdom of fire. Oddly enough
no one welcomed me back, and I'd stand
fully armored as the downpour of cold water
rained down on me and the smoking traces puddled
at my feet like so much milk and melting snow.
Then to disrobe down to my work pants and shirt,
my black street shoes and white cotton socks,
to reassume my nickname, strap on my Bulova,
screw back my wedding ring, and with tap water
gargle away the bitterness as best I could.
For fifteen minutes or more I'd sit quietly
off to the side of the world as the women
polished the tubes and fixtures to a burnished purity
hung like Christmas ornaments on the racks
pulled steadily toward the tanks I'd cooked.
Ahead lay the second cigarette, held in a shaking hand,
as I took into myself the sickening heat to quell heat,

a lunch of two Genoa salami sandwiches and Swiss cheese
on heavy peasant bread baked by my Aunt Tsipie,
and a third cigarette to kill the taste of the others.
Then to arise and dress again in the costume
of my trade for the second time that night, stiffened
by the knowledge that to descend and rise up
from the other world merely once in eight hours is half
what it takes to be known among women and men.

COMING CLOSE

Take this quiet woman, she has been
standing before a polishing wheel
for over three hours, and she lacks
twenty minutes before she can take
a lunch break. Is she a woman?
Consider the arms as they press
the long brass tube against the buffer,
they are striated along the triceps,
the three heads of which clearly show.
Consider the fine dusting of dark down
above the upper lip, and the beads
of sweat that run from under the red
kerchief across the brow and are wiped
away with a blackening wrist band
in one odd motion a child might make
to say No! No! You must come closer
to find out, you must hang your tie
and jacket in one of the lockers
in favor of a black smock, you must
be prepared to spend shift after shift
hauling off the metal trays of stock,
bowing first, knees bent for a purchase,
then lifting with a gasp, the first word
of tenderness between the two of you,
then you must bring new trays of dull,
unpolished tubes. You must feed her,
as they say in the language of the place.
Make no mistake, the place has a language,
and if by some luck the power were cut,
the wheel slowed to a stop so that you
suddenly saw it was not a solid object
but so many separate bristles forming
in motion a perfect circle, she would turn
to you and say, "Why?" Not the old *why*
of *why must I spend five nights a week*?
Just, "Why?" Even if by some magic
you knew, you wouldn't dare speak

for fear of her laughter, which now
you have anyway as she places the five
tapering fingers of her filthy hand
on the arm of your white shirt to mark
you for your own, now and forever.

FIRE

A fire burns along the eastern rim
of mountains. In the valley we
see it as a celestial prank, for
in the summer haze the mountains
themselves are lost, but as the night
deepens the fire grows more golden
and dense. On this calm ground
the raw raging of burning winds
that cuts the eyes and singes the hair
is seen as a pencil-line of light
moving southward. I know my son
is there, has been for four days,
moved in and out by helicopters
with his squad of fire fighters.
By now, without sleep, they've
gone beyond exhaustion. Some can't
waken, some are crazed, a few go
on—the oldest—working steadily.
I know this from the stories he
has told me of other famous fires
from which he returned as from
a dream, his eyes glazed with seeing,
his sense of time and place gone.
He would raise his shaking right arm
above his head, and with his palm
open sweep it toward me again
and again and speak without grammar,
sometimes without words, of what
had taken place. I knew it was true.
Now in the cool of evening I catch
a hint of the forest, of that taking
of sudden breath that pines demand;
it's on my skin, a light oil, a sweat
born of some forgotten leaning into fire.

EVERY BLESSED DAY

First with a glass of water
tasting of iron and then
with more and colder water
over his head he gasps himself
awake. He hears the *cheep*
of winter birds searching
the snow for crumbs of garbage
and knows exactly how much light
and how much darkness is there
before the dawn, gray and weak,
slips between the buildings.
Closing the door behind him,
he thinks of places he
has never seen but heard
about, of the great desert
his father said was like
no sea he had ever crossed
and how at dusk or dawn
it held all the shades of red
and blue in its merging shadows,
and though his life was then
a prison he had come to live
for these suspended moments.
Waiting at the corner he feels
the cold at his back and stamps
himself awake again. Seven miles
from the frozen, narrow river.
Even before he looks he knows
the faces on the bus, some
going to work and some coming back,
but each sealed in its hunger
for a different life, a lost life.
Where he's going or who he is
he doesn't ask himself, he
doesn't know and doesn't know
it matters. He gets off
at the familiar corner, crosses

the emptying parking lots
toward Chevy Gear & Axle # 3.
In a few minutes he will hold
his time card above a clock,
and he can drop it in
and hear the moment crunching
down, or he can not, for
either way the day will last
forever. So he lets it fall.
If he feels the elusive calm
his father spoke of and searched
for all his short life, there's
no way of telling, for now he's
laughing among them, older men
and kids. He's saying, "Damn,
we've got it made." He's
lighting up or chewing with
the others, thousands of miles
from their forgotten homes, each
and every one his father's son.

GROWTH

In the soap factory where I worked
when I was fourteen, I spoke to
no one and only one man spoke
to me and then to command me
to wheel the little cars of damp chips
into the ovens. While the chips dried
I made more racks, nailing together
wood lath and ordinary screening
you'd use to keep flies out, racks
and more racks each long afternoon,
for this was a growing business
in a year of growth. The oil drums
of fat would arrive each morning,
too huge for me to tussle with,
reeking of the dark, cavernous
kitchens of the Greek and Rumanian
restaurants, of cheap hamburger joints,
White Towers and worse. They would
sulk in the battered yard behind
the plant until my boss, Leo,
the squat Ukrainian dollied them in
to become, somehow, through the magic
of chemistry, pure soap. My job
was always the racks and the ovens—
two low ceilinged metal rooms
the color of sick skin. When I
slid open the heavy doors my eyes
started open, the pores
of my skull shrivelled, and sweat
smelling of scared animal burst from
me everywhere. Head down I entered,
first to remove what had dried
and then to wheel in the damp, raw
yellow curls of new soap, grained
like iris petals or unseamed quartz.
Then out to the open weedy yard
among the waiting and emptied drums

where I hammered and sawed, singing
my new life of working and earning,
outside in the fresh air of Detroit
in 1942, a year of growth.

INNOCENCE

Side by side against the trunks of the gray oaks
that lined US 24 we sat while Michelangelo concocted
from tomatoes, hot peppers, onions, salami,
his long blade flashing along the blocks of cheese,
laying the slices precisely down the two slabs
of coarse white bread crafted from a single loaf.
Seriously and in silence we watched, and when he raised
the huge original sandwich to the first bite,
we raised our quarts of milk in a dumb salute
to the sullen gods of time for a thank you
for our mid-day rest. Our Michelangelo was not
the painter, long dead and forgotten by those
beside the road to Toledo during the summer of '50
just before the republic went back to its wars,
but Michelangelo the furious lopper of tree limbs
who leapt all day from branch to leafy branch
to strip those poor old oaks before the earthmovers
dragged them down so that there might be
two smooth new concrete lanes all the way
to the empires of Ohio. (It's there now, the road,
a permanent work of the human imagination,
lined colorfully as all great ways must be,
with the arches of triumph over good taste.)
Each noon Michelangelo told the same joyous tales
of surrender to the 3rd Army Corps in North Africa,
as though he personally had handed over his sword
to Omar Bradley, and then the long sea voyage
to serene Michigan and his second Italian family,
the prosperous cousins in complicated brickwork,
experts in drainage, masters of tree removal
whose thankful apprentice he now was.
We toasted the girls who each night lavished
their cares on his long knotted body topped
perfectly with a roof of black curly thatch.
We even lied back in return, inventing squadrons
of blondes and serious brunettes driven by love
to wait on our doorsteps until we returned

by bus, filthy and broken by the long days
of breaking the earth, women with new cars
and old needs content to take their turns.
Michelangelo would smile, the wise European
come to these innocent shores in a time
of innocence. Later, when the yellow Le Tourneau
earthmovers gripped the chained and stripped trunks,
hunched down and roared their engines, the earth
held and trembled before it gave, and the stumps
howled as they turned their black, prized groins
skyward for the first times in their lives,
turned and rocked back and forth just once
in the heavy wet dirt of late afternoon.
We smiled, not to hide our tears from ourselves
or each other, but because the day was ending,
if there were lamentations they were not ours
but the starlings gathering in the oaks,
the starlings and bobolinks and the vireos
chanting and bowing in the darkening branches
all along the road to Ohio and the coming night.

COMING HOME FROM
THE POST OFFICE

On Sunday night we would
see the women returning
from an evening with God,
their faces glowing with faith
and the hard sweat of their faith.
They would sing separately
or together, and when the bus
stopped and one got carefully
off the sisters would shout
news of the good days ahead
and the joys of handmaidenship.
I remember an evening in April
when I passed in and out of
sleep, and the woman who stood
above me stared into my eyes
as though searching for a sign
that might bring light softly
falling among the dark houses
we stuttered by. When I closed
my eyes I saw cards, letters,
small packages, each bearing
a particular name and some
burden of grief or tidings
of loss. Names like my own
passed moment by moment
into the gray sacks that slumped
open mouthed. On strong legs
she stood easily, swaying
from side to side, a woman
in a green suit, a purse held
in one hand, a hankie folded
in the other. Her pale eyes
held mine easily each time
I wakened, and so I wakened
not into the colorless light
from overhead but into
the twin mysteries of a life

in God. When I fell back
into my light sleep I saw
a great clear river running
between the houses I knew
and a bright shore of temples,
glowing public squares, children
in long robes flowing, those I
loved climbing a high hill
toward a new sun. Hours later
the driver softly wakened
me with a hand on my head
and a single word, and I
stepped lightly into the world,
my shoulders hunched, my collar
turned up against the hour,
and headed down the still street.
The new spring winds groaned
around me, the distant light
of no new star marked me home.

AMONG CHILDREN

I walk among the rows of bowed heads—
the children are sleeping through fourth grade
so as to be ready for what is ahead,
the monumental boredom of junior high
and the rush forward tearing their wings
loose and turning their eyes forever inward.
These are the children of Flint, their fathers
work at the spark plug factory or truck
bottled water in 5 gallon sea-blue jugs
to the widows of the suburbs. You can see
already how their backs have thickened,
how their small hands, soiled by pig iron,
leap and stutter even in dreams. I would like
to sit down among them and read slowly
from *The Book of Job* until the windows
pale and the teacher rises out of a milky sea
of industrial scum, her gowns streaming
with light, her foolish words transformed
into song, I would like to arm each one
with a quiver of arrows so that they might
rush like wind there where no battle rages
shouting among the trumpets, Ha! Ha!
How dear the gift of laughter in the face
of the 8 hour day, the cold winter mornings
without coffee and oranges, the long lines
of mothers in old coats waiting silently
where the gates have closed. Ten years ago
I went among these same children, just born,
in the bright ward of the Sacred Heart and leaned
down to hear their breaths delivered that day,
burning with joy. There was such wonder
in their sleep, such purpose in their eyes
closed against autumn, in their damp heads
blurred with the hair of ponds, and not one
turned against me or the light, not one
said, I am sick, I am tired, I will go home,
not one complained or drifted alone,

unloved, on the hardest day of their lives.
Eleven years from now they will become
the men and women of Flint or Paradise,
the majors of a minor town, and I
will be gone into smoke or memory,
so I bow to them here and whisper
all I know, all I will never know.

WHAT WORK IS

We stand in the rain in a long line
waiting at Ford Highland Park. For work.
You know what work is—if you're
old enough to read this you know what
work is, although you may not do it.
Forget you. This is about waiting,
shifting from one foot to another.
Feeling the light rain falling like mist
into your hair, blurring your vision
until you think you see your own brother
ahead of you, maybe ten places.
You rub your glasses with your fingers,
and of course it's someone else's brother,
narrower across the shoulders than
yours but with the same sad slouch, the grin
that does not hide the stubbornness,
the sad refusal to give in to
rain, to the hours wasted waiting,
to the knowledge that somewhere ahead
a man is waiting who will say, "No,
we're not hiring today," for any
reason he wants. You love your brother,
now suddenly you can hardly stand
the love flooding you for your brother,
who's not beside you or behind or
ahead because he's home trying to
sleep off a miserable night shift
at Cadillac so he can get up
before noon to study his German.
Works eight hours a night so he can sing
Wagner, the opera you hate most,
the worst music ever invented.
How long has it been since you told him
you loved him, held his wide shoulders,
opened your eyes wide and said those words,
and maybe kissed his cheek? You've never
done something so simple, so obvious,

not because you're too young or too dumb,
not because you're jealous or even mean
or incapable of crying in
the presence of another man, no,
just because you don't know what work is.

II

SNAILS

The leaves rusted in the late winds
of September, the ash trees bowed
to no one I could see. Finches
quarrelled among the orange groves.

I was about to say something final
that would capture the meaning
of autumn's arrival, something
suitable for bronzing,

something immediately recognizable
as so large a truth it's totally untrue,
when one small white cloud—not much
more than the merest fragment of mist—

passed between me and the pale
thin cuticle of the mid-day moon
come out to see the traffic and dust
of Central California. I kept quiet.

The wind stilled, and I could hear
the even steady ticking of the leaves,
the lawn's burned hay gasping
for breath, the pale soil rising

only to fall between earth and heaven,
if heaven's there. The world would escape
to become all it's never been
if only we would let it go

streaming toward a future without
purpose or voice. In shade the ground
darkens, and now the silver trails
stretch from leaf to chewed off leaf

of the runners of pumpkin to disappear
in the cover of sheaves and bowed grass.
On the fence blue trumpets of glory
almost closed—music to the moon,

laughter to us, they blared all day
though no one answered, no one
could score their sense or harmony
before they faded in the wind and sun.

MY GRAVE

Just outside Malaga, California,
lost among the cluster of truckstops
there is a little untended plot
of ground and weeds and a stone
that bears my name, misspelled,
and under the stone is dirt, hardpan,
more dirt, rocks, then one hundred
and one different elements
embracing each other in every way
they can imagine so that at times
they remind me of those photographs
I saw as a boy and which I was assured
were expensive and stimulating
and meant nothing. There are also
over a thousand beer bottle caps
one of my sons was saving until
he calculated that he would never
reach a million and so quit. (Quit
saving, not drinking.) One document
is here, ceremoniously labeled
"My Last Will & Testament." My sister
so hated it she threw it into
the bare hole and asked that it be
shovelled under. Not one foolish hope
of mine is here, for none was real
and hard, the hope that the poor
stalked from their cardboard houses
to transform our leaders, that our flags
wept colored tears until they became
nothing but flags of surrender.
I hoped also to see my mother
a long distance runner, my brother
give his money to the kids of Chicago
and take to the roads, carless, hatless,
in search of a task that befits a man.
I dreamed my friends quit lying

and their breath took on the perfume
of new-mown grass, and that I came
to be a man walking carelessly
through rain, my hair tangled, my one
answer the full belly laugh I saved
for my meeting with God, a laugh I
no longer need. Not one nightmare
is here, nor are my eyes which saw
you rise at night, barefoot and quiet,
and leave my side, and my ears which heard
you return suddenly, your mouth tasting
of cold water. Even my forehead
is not here, behind which I plotted
the overthrow of this our republic
by means of the refusal to wipe.
My journals aren't here, my right hand
that wrote them, my waist that strained
against so many leather belts and belts
of cloth that finally surrendered.
My enormous feet that carried me safely
through thirty cities, my tongue
that stroked and restroked your cheek
roughly until you said, "Cat." My poems,
my lies, my few kept promises, my love
for morning sunlight and dusk, my love
for women and the children of women,
my guiding star and the star I wore
for twenty seven years. Nothing of me
is here because this is not my house,
this is not the driver's seat of my car
nor the memory of someone who loved me
nor that distant classroom in which I
fell asleep and dreamed of lamb. This
is dirt, a filled hole of earth, stone
that says return to stone, a broken fence
that mumbles *Keep Out*, air above nothing,

air that cannot imagine the sweet duties
of wildflowers and herbs, this is cheap,
common, coarse, what you pass by
every day in your car without a thought,
this is an ordinary grave.

AGNUS DEI

My little sister created the Lamb of God.
She made him out of used-up dust mops
and coat hangers. She left him whitewashed
at the entrance to the Calvin Coolidge branch
of the public library, so as to scare
the lady librarian who'd clucked at each of us,
"Why do you want to read a grown-up book?"
The lamb sagged against the oaken doors,
high and dark in the deep vault of morning,
and said nothing as we scampered off
across the dew-wet lawns, our shoes darkening.
The rest of our adventure made the *Times*,
how Officer German took in the lamb and made
a morning meal of milk and mucilage
and wrapped him warmly in out-of-town papers.
How he slept unnoticed for hours and wakening
rose in a shower of golden dust, bellowing
in rage, and sent Miss Greenglass running
to the Ladies Restroom where she fainted
and, waking, changed her life. Books scattered.
There was weeping and gnashing. The lamb escaped
through an expensive, leaded windowpane
and entered the late afternoon flying low
over the houses of the middle class
until clouds obscured the world, and it was done.
My brother Leopold read this all out loud
on Sunday morning while our parents slept
above us in a high dark room we never entered,
and the cellar moaned and rumbled, warming
us the best it could. A fresh wind rapped
at the front windows, and we stared in silence
as, bloodred and wrinkled, the new elm unleaved
in public, shuddering with the ache of its growing.

FACTS

The bus station in Princeton, New Jersey,
has no men's room. I had to use one like mad,
but the guy behind the counter said, "Sorry,
but you know what goes on in bus station men's rooms."

If you take a '37 Packard grill and split it down
the center and reduce the angle by 18° and reweld it,
you'll have a perfect grill for a Rolls Royce
just in case you ever need a new grill for yours.

I was not born in Cleveland, Ohio. Other people
were, or so I have read, and many have remained,
which strikes me as an exercise in futility
greater even than saving your pennies to buy a Rolls.

F. Scott Fitzgerald attended Princeton. A student
pointed out the windows of the suite he occupied.
We were on our way to the train station to escape
to New York City, and the student may have been lying.

The train is called "The Dinky." It takes you only
a few miles away to a junction where you can catch
a train to Grand Central or—if you're scared—
to Philadelphia. From either you can reach Cleveland.

My friend Howie wrote me that he was ashamed
to live in a city whose most efficient means of escape
is called "The Dinky." If he'd invest in a Rolls,
even one with a Packard grill, he'd feel differently.

I don't blame the student for lying, especially
to a teacher. He may have been ill at ease
in my company, for I am an enormous man given
to long bouts of silence as I brood on facts.

Facts

There are two lies in the previous stanza. I'm small,
each year I feel the bulk of me shrinking, becoming
more frail and delicate. I get cold easily as though
I lacked even the solidity to protect my own heart.

The coldest I've ever been was in Cleveland, Ohio.
My host and hostess hated and loved each other
by frantic turns. To escape I'd go on long walks
in the yellowing snow as the evening winds raged.

The citizens of Cleveland, Ohio, passed me sullenly,
benighted in their Rolls Royces, each in a halo
of blue light sifting down from the abandoned
filling stations of what once was a community.

I will never return to Cleveland or Princeton, not
even to pay homage to Hart Crane's lonely tower
or the glory days of John Berryman, whom I loved.
I haven't the heart for it. Not even in your Rolls.

GIN

The first time I drank gin
I thought it must be hair tonic.
My brother swiped the bottle
from a guy whose father owned
a drug store that sold booze
in those ancient, honorable days
when we acknowledged the stuff
was a drug. Three of us passed
the bottle around, each tasting
with disbelief. People paid
for this? People had to have
it, the way we had to have
the women we never got near.
(Actually they were girls, but
never mind, the important fact
was their impenetrability.)
Leo, the third foolish partner,
suggested my brother should have
swiped Canadian whiskey or brandy,
but Eddie defended his choice
on the grounds of the expressions
"gin house" and "gin lane," both
of which indicated the preeminence
of gin in the world of drinking,
a world we were entering without
understanding how difficult
exit might be. Maybe the bliss
that came with drinking came
only after a certain period
of apprenticeship. Eddie likened
it to the holy man's self-flagellation
to experience the fullness of faith.
(He was very well read for a kid
of fourteen in the public schools.)
So we dug in and passed the bottle
around a second time and then a third,

in the silence each of us expecting
some transformation. "You get used
to it," Leo said. "You don't
like it but you get used to it."
I know now that brain cells
were dying for no earthly purpose,
that three boys were becoming
increasingly despiritualized
even as they took into themselves
these spirits, but I thought then
I was at last sharing the world
with the movie stars, that before
long I would be shaving because
I needed to, that hair would
sprout across the flat prairie
of my chest and plunge even
to my groin, that first girls
and then women would be drawn
to my qualities. Amazingly, later
some of this took place, but
first the bottle had to be
emptied, and then the three boys
had to empty themselves of all
they had so painfully taken in
and by means even more painful
as they bowed by turns over
the eye of the toilet bowl
to discharge their shame. Ahead
lay cigarettes, the futility
of guaranteed programs of
exercise, the elaborate lies
of conquest no one believed,
forms of sexual torture and
rejection undreamed of. Ahead
lay our fifteenth birthdays,
acne, deodorants, crabs, salves,
butch haircuts, draft registration,

the military and political victories
of Dwight Eisenhower, who brought us
Richard Nixon with wife and dog.
Any wonder we tried gin.

PERENNIALS

Winter. The marketplace of the village
of Fuengirola. A tattered mongrel,
tan, brown, and black with a white muzzle.
The stubby, bowed forelegs set apart
in a stance suitable for a short advance
or a sudden retreat. I know this beast,
I think, I know this dirty, box-like head
ringed with curls, this dry, foolish bark
that scares off nothing. "Marilyn," I say,
remembering one who scorned me years before.
Each day my son John calls out, "Marilyn!"
as stamping we wait our turn in line
before the black oildrums of burning fat
where the *churros* fry. "Marilyn," he calls
until she comes to beg bread from his hand.

*

Under the windows onto the gray yard
a green glass wine bottle with one branch
of blood-tipped bursting plum. The odor
of mid-summer hanging in winter.
The room thickens around the living core
as I pass and stop. Where was I going
that I should ignore the heart of my house,
this new intruder come in another
dark season to tell me the year won't wait?
I was on the way to the kitchen
for a glass of water, and now I have wine.
I was looking for a brown paper sack
of sleep, an old pillow of forgetting,
a way out before the world got in,
and found the dining room in riot
from one black branch as arched as I.

ABOVE THE WORLD

Up through miles of twisting pines, past
a town of brightly painted caves, their windows
curtained and open, the doors ajar revealing
the heavy furniture of entrepreneurs, carpets,
television sets; on the roofs, antennas poking
in all directions and the day's laundry strung
from cave to cave. Up another hour or more
winding through dense woods to a high plateau,
then truck farms greening in December, fenced
fields of grazing cattle right to the outskirts
of the new town, raw, unfinished, with wide streets
of crowded shops hawking garter belts, canes,
fountain pens, goatskin jackets, peeled rabbits.
The women, in dark print dresses, clutched
their leather purses with both hands, the men
smoked in small circles. At the center, a maze
of wires and tracks sprouting from a compound
of ancient trolleys leaning into silence,
their windows gone, the cane seats unravelling,
the paint cracked and flaking. One road led
up the mountain, and we took it and left
the trucks, the clouds of black soot, the roar
of motorcycles to enter something
far older, and found the place and parked.
We registered at the Hotel of Heaven,
a father, a mother, three upright blond sons
in American jeans, blue-eyed and suspicious.
Would my kids now remember the parapets
that hung out over the edge of the world
that spread before us—the fabled Mare Nostrum
we never saw—as everything below dissolved
in smoke and dust? The tangled gardens
of a long-gone magistrate, their paths clogged
with weeds, the roses blown and climbing
everywhere, the famous court of stone lions
each as large and fierce as a happy dog,
each facing away from his brothers to guard

nothing from no one. Even the tall, graying
Englishman stooped before his easel was not
a dream, nor was the painting itself, still
largely canvas, though it caught the green
exactly, shadowed with black, and a sky
of distant clouds, small and bored,
floating away. That man would be ninety
or older now and still at the task
of rendering the magic and nonsense of lives
lived at great height, still not answering
the unanswerable questions of high mist,
brain cells fighting for breath, our bondage
to a line of perfect crows marking the way up.
Make no mistake, for even here you could still
go up along ragged stone trails that wound
their way into a gray world and from there
into thin air. Or you could descend
in summer to the music of water on the narrow
cobbled streets, or in silent December,
as we did, the mother leading the way,
the father taking up the rear in Spanish style,
laboring over a newspaper of local filth.
There was darkness. It fell even before
the cold fell, even before the late sun
vanished behind the mountains, it fell
into the corners of sight slowly
like stained snow. In the restaurant
there was more cold and darkness. A fine layer
of dust had settled on plates and silverware.
I wondered if anyone else saw it
sifting down but was scared to ask. One rear door
stood open on the night, though no animals
entered or left. We sent the soup back,
a clear broth of boiled water dotted
with islands of fat. We tried the bread
that gleamed like old china, we even tried
the thin burned steaks. We tried. And then

we walked the streets to a little square
where the children sold white paper dolls
you could explode with a lighted cigarette
and necklaces of wooden beads meant
for Christmas angels, who were sure to come,
for everything is answered in the Old World,
the Gypsy peddler told us as he wrapped
the chestnuts six to a triangled pack,
his stubby burned fingers working deftly.
"Everything!" he promised. I turned away
from the laughter and threats, turned away
from my wife and kids. Suddenly alone,
believing he was right, I turned to behold
the sky I'd always lived under bulging
with huge, unfamiliar stars closer
than I'd ever seen them and moving, frozen,
in that ancient, secret dance. Who could
have guessed how everything was answered
before the night ended? At the hotel a room
for each of us, windowless and sealed,
a private cell for sleep or prayer,
and seven more for those who never came—
a dozen tiny rooms in all, circling
a low-ceilinged common room that held
one great round table with attendant chairs,
equitably, as they never are in this life.
Beside the table and below the portrait
of God, the iron stove a boy filled with twigs,
broken crates, garbage, while we watched.
This, too, was answered. The grandfather,
smiling sideways at his audience, lit the blaze
and leaped back, laughing, for even here
above the world we would have all that night,
even unto the clear break of day, steam heat.

M. DEGAS TEACHES ART & SCIENCE
AT DURFEE INTERMEDIATE SCHOOL
Detroit, 1942

He made a line on the blackboard,
one bold stroke from right to left
diagonally downward and stood back
to ask, looking as always at no one
in particular, "What have I done?"
From the back of the room Freddie
shouted, "You've broken a piece
of chalk." M. Degas did not smile.
"What have I done?" he repeated.
The most intellectual students
looked down to study their desks
except for Gertrude Bimmler, who raised
her hand before she spoke. "M. Degas,
you have created the hypotenuse
of an isosceles triangle." Degas mused.
Everyone knew that Gertrude could not
be incorrect. "It is possible,"
Louis Warshowsky added precisely,
"that you have begun to represent
the roof of a barn." I remember
that it was exactly twenty minutes
past eleven, and I thought at worst
this would go on another forty
minutes. It was early April,
the snow had all but melted on
the playgrounds, the elms and maples
bordering the cracked walks shivered
in the new winds, and I believed
that before I knew it I'd be
swaggering to the candy store
for a Milky Way. M. Degas
pursed his lips, and the room
stilled until the long hand
of the clock moved to twenty one
as though in complicity with Gertrude,

who added confidently, "You've begun
to separate the dark from the dark."
I looked back for help, but now
the trees bucked and quaked, and I
knew this could go on forever.

III

BURNED

I have to go back into the forge room
at Chevy where Lonnie still calls
out his commands to Sweet Pea and Packy
and stare into the fire
until my eyes are also fire
and tear away some piece of my face
because we're all burning in the blood
and it's too late.
                  I have to walk
the long road from here to Bessemer,
Alabama, and arrive on a June night in '48
after work when the men have crowded
around a stalled car and tell them
there's no place to go and
let them take turns beating me
with hands turned to pig iron.
                        I have to
climb the shaking ladder to the roof
of the Nitro/plant and tear off
my respirator and breathe the yellow air
the Chaldeans called "the air you must not breathe,"
and sing in the voices
of my fathers calling the children
into prayer while below the stubby canisters
pass labelled, "Chicago," "Amsterdam,"
"Belsen," "Toronto."
                   I have to swim out
into the flat waters of the great sea
at dawn when the small fishing boats
are coming in and climb aboard the one
with the face of a goddess and the tail
of a goat and let my left cheek
brush against the rough, unshaven cheek
of the old man whose tears—mixed with wine—
watered the beach twenty one years ago.
                          And
keep going past the last marker

until I am lost forever, until the sea
and the sky are one, the waves have ceased,
no tide pulls us toward
the cries of the drowned.
                              I have to climb
the slag hills again, but this time not
as a child, and look out over the river of iron,
and hold it all in my eyes,
the river, the iron mountains, the factories
where our brothers burned. I have to repeat
the prayer that we will all go back
to earth one day soon to become earth,
that our tears will run to the sea
a last time and open it, and our fires
light the way back home for someone.

                    *

In the fullness of a season someone
had to go first into the other kingdom.
Summer in Detroit. The light scattered
into tiny flares at the end of a day
of hard work. Stanley walked his dog,
talking as always to himself, Dorothy
sat on the front porch alone, excited
by the knowledge of her changing body.
Blocks away Leo read *The Tempest* slowly
to himself, stopping now and then to announce
a line out loud— "Thy turfy mountains
where live nibbling sheep"—, his skin
chilled with the glory of language.
I have not brought them together
so their hearts might stutter or stop
with love they can't bear. It is 1944,
Moradian has landed on a Pacific atoll
to become his life forever, Esther's husband
sees the Sherman twenty yards ahead

go up in a flash and knows his is next.
Past midnight Bernard and Arthur vow
to give themselves to music and to poetry.
I do not call out, I do not step forward
out of the chaos of my 16 years to ask
to take their place. I'm too young,
too exhausted, too busy. In the kitchen
I stand at the counter slicing cheese,
salami, rye bread, spreading mayonnaise,
tamping down the lettuce, wrapping
the sandwiches carefully in waxed paper
for tomorrow's lunch the exact way
my grandmother taught me years before,
humming one of my grandfather's tunes,
one he groans out when he sings himself
to sleep, tapping his foot, swinging
from side to side as though he were burning.

*

A burned car left in a field
of sassafras, the long green shoots
through the windows and doors where no
doors remain. The kids don't come by
after school to carve their names
on the dashboard or pull the steering wheel
to avoid the inevitable. Rocks, tires,
cases of empties, an old couch sagging
into weeds, the cushions blooming.
I lived here once, in a house
now gone. A friend visited me
at dusk, and she brought a paper parcel
of cookies tied with a ribbon. Even then
we were scared of the silence that followed
whatever we gave each other. I would
walk her to the bus stop on Second Avenue,
and we'd wait in silence in the dense air

of a March night as slow rain
fell into the last snow. I'd come back
alone, sober, singing to a starless sky,
singing recklessly out of a boy's
throat, past the darkened rows
of sleeping two storey houses
that have all gone up in smoke.

*

Yom Kippur
in the New World.
Los Angeles hums
a little tune—
trucks down
the coast road
for Monday market
packed with small faces
blinking in the dark.
My mother dreams
by the open window.
On the drainboard
the gray roast humps
untouched, the oven
bangs its iron jaws,
but it's over.
Before her on the table
set for so many
her glass of fire
goes out.
The childish photographs,
the letters and cards
scatter at last.
The dead burn alone
toward dawn.

*

Why am I going away from the glass of wine
from the loaf of bread
Why am I not mourning the tiny death
of the sparrow
who leaped on the lowest branches
of the atlas cedar
until one afternoon he was drawn
into tall burning grass
What will I say when the nights grow
longer and longer
the dawn is barely visible, a grudging
of yellow light
The day dies into the violet halos
of exhaust
No one takes my hand and leads me to bed
to the mouth to mouth agonies of darkness
When this passes
how will I know I was and I was alive
Who will take my hand
smelling of earth and
burning now to autumnal rust
Who will lead me to the ceremonies of sorrow
who will lead me

*

I was burned,
she said, and lifted her blouse to show
me the curious pale mottling along
the lines of her belly, still smooth. "He
said he adored my white skin, creamy.
Can a Jew imagine what a real
white woman looks like all over? All
your life you dream of someone like me,
every night of your life." Her green eyes

47

on fire with her own memories
of herself 40 years ago. She shakes her head
awake and still goes on. "Not with cigarettes,
you moron, would a man like that, richer
than God, burn his only beloved with
cigarettes? Cigars, imported Havanas, nothing
but the best!"
                    And she's gone, thank God,
slamming the door on me, gone back
to the one life she clings to. The room
is quiet, ashamed, the books gawk down
from their shelves, not one
with a word to tell me what it is like
to enter the fires of your own making, naked,
day after day, until the burning becomes
a sweetness.

*

                The day you left I walked
alone for hours down the crowded streets
hearing and seeing no one until I
caught the cries of a drunken woman
behind me. She had lost her husband,
left him in a bar, was alone, frightened,
calling for help. I kept walking
with her behind me, calling.
The houses along the canals were closing
up, turning their eyes inward,
listening to the rumbling of their fires
or their human groans. This day will end,
I told myself, this pain will pass.
I will waken to my life. The evening
spread from the great oaks
that lined the emptying boulevards
or descended in bits of ashes and dust
from a deepening sky. I turned at last

to behold the woman whose grief
was louder than mine. There was
only a child, her right hand closed
tight on a handkerchief, knotted at one end
with some coins and a note, a little girl
who seeing my eyes filled with tears
began to cry as she smiled.

*

Two ten-inch phonograph records, *Bluebirds*,
going white, that won't give up their music.
My uncle's perfect cloth bound book
that opened the secret of electric growth.
My mother's gap-toothed tortoise combs.
My father's Victoria Cross he brought back
from an automobile parts convention
in Chicago. His white gold pocket watch,
a Howard, that runs and stops and runs
to keep his time. His naturalization papers
claiming he was born in 1898 in Poland,
without a single mention of his years at war.
My brother's smeared grade school drawings
of Spitfires, Stukas, ME 109s,
his "Withdrawal from Dunkirk," the beach
crisscrossed with small black lines
that could be abandoned arms or the arms
of boys hugging. My stillborn sister's
wish to walk with us on Sunday afternoons,
to breathe the stained air that blows
in at dusk from the parking lots,
to mother a child. Your finger prints
on the final application for release.
A bitten fountain pen, a dry stamp pad.
Two clear drops of fluid that catch
and hold the artificial light, that glow
with their own light when that's gone

as eyes in stories are said to do.
Now in the dark they could be you,
they could be me, they could be anyone.

*

I stop at the borders of dreams.
I ask who you are, whispering
in my ear all these years, you
to whom I've said all I can say.
I hold my two hands upward
toward the light now sifting
from the air. That is the shape
of eternity: five long fingers
and a palm broadened and carved
by use. When I looked
in my heart and found only
questions, when I walked
beside the ditch at dusk
and asked the sun,
the answer was curled
quietly in my pocket. "Look at
them both," you say, "turn them
over and place them on the table
before you. Don't be afraid.
They are you, familiar, at times
overlooked, despised. Now,
go back the way you came, down
the same old streets where you
grew to a name and a single face.
That was home, you said, and today
it is nothing, not even a closet
of unread books. Here is home.
Close your eyes. You are on
a dark plain. The hot winds
breathe in and out. You're laughing!
You asked for a home, you crossed

the earth, you sat speechless,
you questioned the closed door,
'Are you there?' No one answered
because all the time it was you."

*

If I called you "my soul," you'd
laugh in my face. If I went
down on my knees to you as to
a god or a beloved, you'd turn
to the window, shake your head,
and talk to the last of the garden.
At the end of September I may
ask the trees to hold still
in the west wind. I may scold
the flicker hiding in the shade
of an orange tree. His feathers
scatter and settle in the trough
of each wave. He is not
a religious object nor is
the wind sacred, smelling
as it does of cold salt
and sea life. I have been here
so long the bleached hairs
quivering on my hands remember
the years before the flood.
The whites of my eyes, no longer
white, stared into fire when fire
was mine, and I am only
so much salt, water, and stone
smelling of iron. I can talk
to you and though my answers
will scatter like feathers in wind,
you may write them down on paper
that burns even in sunlight.
Get what you can, says the flicker;

remorseless, he shoulders his way
into light and then into air.
What does he care that the year
winds down? That the west wind
smells of ice? That what went out
as lies and so much bad breath
came home as the final truth?

*

The outskirts of our least favorite city,
the one bombed and burned from the inside
by its own citizens—along the fence
small climbing roses bloom in April,
the hardier ones hang on long
past the better days, and late autumn
brings tiny crystals glistening
on the cheeks of the blackened petals.
Spading the gray soil, I think
of begonias and how their buds redden
even without rain and of the wild iris—
flags we called them—that won't live
in the rich beds though they survive
fire and hail outbattling tough weeds
to spring up where houses once were.
Poking among these ruins for rocks
for the garden, I unearth bricks
from a familiar fireplace or a slab
of stone that crowned a hearth, remnants
of my lost neighbors. Spilling
the kernels of carrot seeds
into my palm and the black pips
of radishes, I know something
will come from this root and wood
thickened ground. With a stick I scrape
a trough for planting. I remember
the unloved lamb become a sheep I saw

on his way to slaughter. Like me, he shook
his lowered head as though he knew
the way home, that head dirty with curls.

*

I was small once, hardly bigger
than the laughter of a lemon and like
a lemon I had come into a life
no one would question, an oily rind,
closed volumes of flesh, and seeds
as smooth as pearls. Even then
you could talk, you were immense
with the desire to touch each leaf,
each small animal that rose
from his lair. Later,
even you who could love rind,
seeds, oil, flesh, let your name
slip from your tongue to become
nonsense, let salt rain down
into the fields and surrendered
all you'd seen, you who had
eaten the earth gave back ashes.
So, it is time we left.
Take the small, empty purse
your mother carried across an ocean,
take the little book of songs
the children taught you, take
your teeth and your fingernails
and the white scars on your belly
and meet me where the road
vanishes into the hillside.
How will you know me?
I won't be tall or dressed
for dinner or carrying a dark bag,
I won't be whistling like a bird
or your father coming home from work,

I won't be anyone you ever
spoke to or fell asleep beside
or wakened to. I won't be sorry
for you, I won't take your hand
or come forward and touch
your hair or kiss your cheek.
There, between the two sullen elms
without leaves, the ones that died
years ago, do you see a shadow?
It could be the birth we gave
back to the rain. It could be
the silence after love or just pain
without hope or the need to dance.
It looks alive, even in the darkness,
it looks as though it were growing
smaller and smaller, but it's
not a patch of snow. It could be
a whisper, a secret never kept,
everything your heart knew
and you forgot. Don't ask.

*

Give me your hand, and I'll count
each finger twice and put them to sleep
with a name more cold and remote
than a star's. They don't move,
not even to breathe, not even
to search for water or to embrace
another hand. This is the way
things become as we return closer
and closer to air that simply is,
stained by a day not yet here.

A woman gets out of bed and goes
to the window to see if the birds
have wakened and sees the houses

have gone, the trees have turned
inward to become so many pages
unmarked by mistakes. She says
nothing to herself. She makes the bed
and washes the one plate, the cup,
the little spoon and fork. She dries
them carefully and lets them fall
one by one into the garbage.

*

                     Here it comes.
It's been quiet. If you'd bothered
you'd have heard finches in the trees
and the wind sighing out back and wires
humming in the voices of wire, you
could have heard a country asleep
except for the people down under
stoking the furnaces and the ones
way up changing the light bulbs.
No more. Because here it is,
the big wave the moon's been holding
back and the Rocky Mountains
of ice water. Now the clouds of locusts
waiting since *Genesis* sweep over Kansas
and eat wheat and carry off the cows.
And the constant hum? It's California
on its knees chanting to keep safe
our vintage wines and swimming pools,
the false Gods of our movies
and the true dead ones in our hearts.
Los Angeles, Seattle, New York City,
Detroit, Washington, gone to sea.
Now you can hear again, finches
in the golden voices of finch, the wind
saying it best as only the old wind
can, blowing over the centuries of nothing,
blowing every which way it wants, blowing.

*

Once in a park in Paris an old woman
seized two coins nesting on my open palm.
I grabbed the offending hand, closed
now like a tiny steel cage, and twisted
while she gasped and tore at my hand
with her nails. At last one dark tear
dripped from her nose and the two coins fell
into the grass. When I put a shoe over them
she cried to the low clouds scudding overhead
that all men were strangers and sons of whores.
Leaving the coins, I stood and walked away.
I did not have to turn to know that smile—
I'd seen it on my own face, I'd known
the same hump in my shoulders, the cold
gleaming in my eyes, and wanted not to see.
"What if grass were bread?" my son asked me
a week before when the plane broke through
the dense rain and we beheld the green world.
I had no answer. When we landed
I bought money with money, forgetting
that each dollar spent was so much time
staring into faces that answered nothing.
Later, in the hotel, my kids played
with the elevator until the old concierge
hissed at them in French, and they roared
out the laughter of boys and refused to stop.
When he came to my door to complain
I answered that in the West grass was bread.
He held his pudgy hands over his breast
to deliver his truths of waste and use.
How many years had he gone faithfully
from room to room turning out lights,
searching for loose change? How many days
had he ended by reheating lunch and praying?
I consider the long fields that blaze

in early March across the lower hills
of the great Sierras. I cannot answer.
I remember a warm bakery in winter north
of the village of Lorca where I bought bread,
the women smiling at me and giving me
the first place in line. Bread so stale
it shattered into shards as sharp as glass
when we tried to break it. My kids,
my wife, and I howled with glee.
The father had returned, his face full
of trust, bearing the gifts of earth.
It was afternoon, cold, and we had hours to go,
we had sour red wine and empty stomachs.

*

                     To enter the fire
is to be burned, said Leo Maryk, slumped
on the loading dock behind Kelsey-Hayes.
He'd read it somewhere, maybe the Epistles
of Paul or one of the early Fathers,
Augustine or Ambrose. On a night like this
they all ran together in his head.
"Some kind of priest I'll make," he laughed.
Even in the cold I could see the sweat
running down the long, jagged nose, the steam
rising from his enormous chest as from
an oven as he clenched and unclenched
his gloved hands. "A man the size
of me terrified of every little woman,
afraid to live the life my father lived,
I even changed my name." Marikowski asking me
what was love if he couldn't feel it
with his body? what was it? Asking me,
a kid more ignorant than he. Above us a low sky,
the slag heaps burning slowly toward a day
that never came, the others—men and women—

passing in and out of the same fires
they never saw into the world.

*

Once I believed I lived these closed
rows of tenements, the shotgunned houses
bunched uselessly against the coming
of another day. Now the stars settle
down, easing themselves into the river.
Shivering with delight, they almost
go out, but a high wind fans the little
separate points of flame. An ore boat
passes upriver. Riding soundlessly
the other way, another parts the waters
toward seven oceans and an older world.

*

The slow windward motion of the stars.
Late rain falling for hours
between the squat, closed houses.
Then silence, the town asleep, the light
not yet arrived where a single shade is torn
or a door leans ajar. A wagon pulled
down the bricked alley, and there is milk,
bread in cold packages, white, untouched.

Imagine the darkness drawn away,
the new day falling equitably
in the valleys of the living. Imagine
all the long morning fathers rising
with their wives, children making way
for children at sink and table on a day
without work or school until dusk
shatters the golden windows.
Imagine it.

*

The first time we entered
the city, it was late afternoon, Friday,
behind miles of trucks and old cars spewing
everywhere. Past closed warehouses
of gray cotton cloth, factories, low-built
laboratories grinding out antibiotics
and corn plasters. Each time the traffic
stalled we sat in stunned silence. This
would be home. Before long we
found a room and entered the darkness
together, holding each other
as long as we could in the hope
we would be home.
                          Morning. On the streets
a tiny man leans back planting
his heels as six greyhounds tug him
toward the single tree. Our old friends
the sparrows busy in the gutters turning
yesterday's papers for a hint of the truth.
A blue sky enters from nowhere. A truck
delivers oranges and red sacks of milk.
Air so clear I can see all the way down
the Ramblas to where the sea goes out
on its one voyage, all the way up
to the Holy Mountain from which the devil
said, "Behold, it shall be yours, all
the kingdoms below," and we made our choice.

*

Rain falling into the dry canals
east of here. Old couches, magazines,
dinettes—their legs skyward—, car seats
unstick slowly from the gray mud and drift

spinning toward the little dams and weirs.
A skirt, stained with wine or blood, fills
with water and swirls to the surface,
a carton of empty beer cans like trophies.
A black setter comes toward me, springing
easily along the bank, his long head
hung low, his coat soaked and heavy,
and passes without a sign.
                              Another day.
The sun still up past six, the dark clouds
gone into the foothills or farther,
the clear sky darkening. The water
moves swiftly past islands of calm
and darkness. I glimpse a root, bare
and silvery, groping upward through air,
an open hand of black branches breaks
the surface for a moment and then
turns under and closes up. Somewhere
a light comes on in a living room,
someone I don't know pauses at
the window before the last light goes
and speaks to me.
                      One great room, the moon
sliding through the trailing wisps
of clouds or dust clouds. The child
gone under in clear water years ago,
the sad yelps of brothers and sisters
that went on and on until morning
quiet at last. The earth's own sighs,
the day's last breath going out,
my own silent cry of denial. They're
all asleep, all the windows from here
to the end of the world are open,
I can hear the even breathing
of all that is wordless and final.

IV

SOLOING

My mother tells me she dreamed
of John Coltrane, a young Trane
playing his music with such joy
and contained energy and rage
she could not hold back her tears.
And sitting awake now, her hands
crossed in her lap, the tears start
in her blind eyes. The TV set
behind her is gray, expressionless.
It is late, the neighbors quiet,
even the city—Los Angeles—quiet.
I have driven for hours down 99,
over the Grapevine into heaven
to be here. I place my left hand
on her shoulder, and she smiles.
What a world, a mother and son
finding solace in California
just where we were told it would
be, among the palm trees and all-
night super markets pushing orange
back-lighted oranges at 2 A.M.
"He was alone," she says, and does
not say, just as I am, "soloing."
What a world, a great man half
her age comes to my mother
in sleep to give her the gift
of song, which—shaking the tears
away—she passes on to me, for now
I can hear the music of the world
in the silence and that word:
soloing. What a world—when I
arrived the great bowl of mountains
was hidden in a cloud of exhaust,
the sea spread out like a carpet
of oil, the roses I had brought
from Fresno browned on the seat
beside me, and I could have
turned back and lost the music.

SCOUTING

I'm the man who gets off the bus
at the bare junction of nothing
with nothing, and then heads back
to where we've been as though
the future were stashed somewhere
in that tangle of events we call
"Where I come from." Where I
came from the fences ran right
down to the road, and the lone woman
leaning back on her front porch as she
quietly smoked asked me what did
I want. Confused as always, I
answered, "Water," and she came to me
with a frosted bottle and a cup,
shook my hand, and said, "Good luck."
That was forty years ago, you say,
when anything was possible. No,
it was yesterday, the gray icebox
sat on the front porch, the crop
was tobacco and not yet in, you
could hear it sighing out back.
The rocker gradually slowed as
she came toward me but never
stopped and the two of us went on
living in time. One of her eyes
had a pale cast and looked nowhere
or into the future where without
regrets she would give up the power
to grant life, and I would darken
like wood left in the rain and then
fade into only a hint of the grain.
I went higher up the mountain
until my breath came in gasps,
my sight darkened, and I slept
to the side of the road to waken

chilled in the sudden July cold,
alone and well. What is it like
to come to, nowhere, in darkness,
not knowing who you are, not
caring if the wind calms, the stars
stall in their sudden orbits,
the cities below go on without
you, screaming and singing?
I don't have the answer. I'm
scouting, getting the feel
of the land, the way the fields
step down the mountainsides
hugging their battered, sagging
wire fences to themselves as though
both day and night they needed
to know their limits. Almost still,
the silent dogs wound into sleep,
the gray cabins breathing steadily
in moonlight, tomorrow wakening
slowly in the clumps of mountain oak
and pine where streams once ran
down the little white rock gullies.
You can feel the whole country
wanting to waken into a child's dream,
you can feel the moment reaching
back to contain your life and forward
to whatever the dawn brings you to.
In the dark you can love this place.

COMING OF AGE IN MICHIGAN

New Year's Eve, 1947, the old one's ending
or the new beginning on a familiar note.
His name is McDonald, his father owns a dairy
down the block from Brass Craft where I polish
flexible plumbing tubes by the hour. "Sol and Abie,"
he says, "Fe're not open yet for bizniz," then holds
his nose against that awful smell, the "Abie" smell
no one asked for. Noel Baker begins to cry.

How did the night end? I can't remember it ending.
I can remember counting the house, an even dozen
of them and two of us. My brother threw his drink
against the wall, and no one moved on him, no one
said a thing. McDonald was dragged off laughing
to a bedroom in his fancy suite we'd been invited
into by some genuine innocent who didn't know
a Jew from Commodore Vanderbilt without his yacht.

I remember my joy at seeing Noel Baker for the first time
since the 8th grade, a skinny whiz at math and English
in penny loafers and monogrammed sweaters. (I saw her
only once after that in a liquor store in early June
years later, she was talking too much and too loudly,
but he didn't mind, he'd left the motor running—
a white LaSalle convertible they floated off in
while we waited in line.) I forget all the rest.

*

Have I taken something away from you? Noel Baker
did not become a famous woman: it was too late
to enter the fiction of F. Scott Fitzgerald, too early
for her to become the governor of Michigan,
which hardly makes you famous. My brother and I
did not throw McDonald from a 7th story window
of the Book Cadillac and into *The Detroit Free Press*,
we did not even have the good taste to have our teeth

knocked loose, to come home with our best white shirts
blood smeared, our ties torn to shreds, cigarettes
dangling from swollen lips. Don't blame us.
The Book Cadillac is still going, though it smells
like a steam bath, and the rooms are tiny and gray.
(Down the boulevard the Statler, boarded over and serene,
did not compromise, the Fox Theatre around the corner—
a rip-off of the great mosque of Cordoba—became

a car park, and even the bus station got up one morning
and moved to the suburbs.) No one that night turned
into literature, nothing that we did or didn't
entered the mythology of boys growing into men
or girls fighting to be people. Everyone went home
because that was how the world was before God
tuned to prime-time TV and kids still rose early
to catch the bus for school and everyone was innocent.

THE RIGHT CROSS

The sun rising over the mountains
found me awake, found an entire valley
of sleepers awake, dreaming of a few hours
more of sleep. Though the Great Central Valley
is home for the homeless, the fruit pickers
of creation, for runaway housewives
bored by their husbands, and bored husbands,
the rising sun does not dip back behind
the Sierras until we're ready. The Valley sun
just comes on. We rise, drop our faces
in cold water, and face the prospects
of a day like the last one from which we
have not recovered. All this month I've
gone in search of the right cross, the punch
which had I mastered it forty years ago
might have saved me from the worst. The heavy bag
still hangs from the rafters of the garage,
turning in no wind, where my youngest son
left it when he went off ten years ago
abandoning his childish pursuits to me.
After tea, dry toast, and some toe-touching,
I'm ready to work. I pull on the salty
bag gloves, bow my head, dip one shoulder

into the great sullen weight, and begin
with a series of quick jabs. I'm up
on my toes, moving clockwise, grunting
as the blows crumple, the air going out
and coming back in little hot benedictions.
I'm remembering Nate Coleman barking
all those years ago, "Straight from the shoulder,
Levine," as though describing his own nature.
The gentlest man I ever knew, perfect
with his fists, our master and mentor,
who fought only for the love of it,

living secretly by day in suit and tie,
vending copper cookware from the back seat
of his black Plymouth. The dust rises
from the sour bag, and I feel how fragile
my left wrist has become, how meek the bones
of my shoulders as the shocks come home,
the bag barely moving. "Let it go!"
Nate would call, urging the right hand out
against the big light heavies, Marvin
with his sudden feints and blunt Becker,
his face grim and closed behind cocked fists.
Later, the gym gone silent in the half-dark,
Nate would stand beside me, left hand
on my shoulder, and take my right wrist
loosely in his right hand, and push it out
toward an imagined foe, his right knee
pressed behind my right knee until my leg
came forward. I could feel his words
—"like this"—falling softly on my cheek
and smell the milky sweetness of his breath
—"you just let it go"—, the dark lashes
of his mysterious green eyes unmoving.
The bag is going now, swinging easily
with the force of jabs and hooks. The garage
moans as though this dance at its center
threatened to bring it down. I throw a right,
another, and another before I take my rest
in the cleared space amid the detritus
of five lives: boxes of unanswered letters,
school papers, report cards, scattered parts
of lawn mowers and motorcycles gone to ground.
The sky is coming through the mismatched boards
of the roof, pure blue and distant, the day
rising from the oily cement of the floor
as again I circle the heavy bag throwing out
more punches until I can't. If my sons
were here they'd cheer me on, and I'd

keep going into the impossible heat
and before I quit I might throw, just once,
for the first time, the perfect right cross.
They say it's magic. When it lands
you feel the force of your whole body,
even the deeper organs, the dark fluids
that go untapped for decades, the tiny
pale microbes haunting the bone marrow,
the intricate patterns that devised
the bones of the feet, you feel them
finally coming together like so many
atoms of salt and water as they form
an ocean or a tear, for just an instant
before the hand comes back under the chin
in its ordinary defensive posture.
The boys, the grown men dreaming
of the squared circle into which the light
falls evenly as they move without effort
hour after hour, breathing easily, oiled
with their own sweat, fight for nothing
except the beauty of their own balance,
the precision of each punch.
I hated to fight. I saw each blow
in a sequence of events leading
finally to a winner and a loser.
Yet I fought as boys were told to do,
and won and lost as men must. That's over.
Six months from my sixtieth year, doused
in my own juices, I call it quits
for the day, having earned the rituals—
the long bath, the shave, the laundered clothes,
the afternoon muse as the little clots
of stiffness break up and travel down
the channels of the blood. After dinner
and before sleep, I walk behind the garage
among grape vines and swelling tomatoes
to where the morning glories close down

in the rising darkness and the cosmos
flare their brilliant whites a last time
before the moon comes out. From under
the orange trees the click and chuckle
of quail; the tiny chicks dart out
for a last look and scurry back again
before the earth goes gray. A dove moans,
another answers from a distant yard as though
they called each other home, called each of us
back to our beds for the day's last work.

THE SWEETNESS OF BOBBY HEFKA

What do you make of little Bobby Hefka
in the 11th grade admitting to Mr. Jaslow
that he was a racist and if Mr. Jaslow
was so tolerant how come he couldn't
tolerate Bobby? The class was stunned.
"How do you feel about the Jews?"
asked my brother Eddie, menacingly.
"Oh, come on, Eddie," Bobby said,
"I thought we were friends." Mr. Jaslow
banged the desk to regain control.
"What is it about Negroes you do not like?"
he asked in his most rational voice,
which always failed to hide the fact
he was crazy as a bed bug, claiming
Capek's *RUR* was far greater than *Macbeth*.
Bobby was silent for a long minute, thinking.
"Negroes frighten me," he finally said,
"they frighten my mother and father who never
saw them in Finland, they scare my brother
who's much bigger than me." Then he added
the one name, Joe Louis, who had been
busy cutting down black and white men
no matter what their size. Mr. Jaslow
sighed with compassion. We knew that
before the class ended he'd be telling us
a great era for men and women was imminent
if only we could cross the threshold
into humanitarianism, into the ideals
of G. B. Shaw, Karel Capek, and Mr. Jaslow.
I looked across the room to where Bobby
sat in the back row next to the windows.
He was still awake, his blue eyes wide.
Beyond him the dark clouds of 1945
were clustering over Linwood, the smokestack
of the power plant gave its worst
to a low sky. Lacking the patience to wait
for combat, Johnny Mooradian had quit school

a year before, and Johnny was dead on an atoll
without a name. Bobby Hefka had told the truth
—to his own shame and pride—and the rains
came on. Nothing had changed for a roomful
of 17 year olds more scared of life than death.
The last time I saw Bobby Hefka he was driving
a milk truck for Dairy Cream, he was married,
he had a little girl, he still dreamed
of going to medical school. He listened
in sorrow to what had become of me. He handed
me an icy quart bottle of milk, a gift
we both held on to for a silent moment
while the great city roared around us, the trucks
honking and racing their engines to make him move.
His eyes were wide open. Bobby Hefka loved me.

ON THE RIVER

My brother has an old row boat
moored to a dock at the foot
of Jefferson Avenue, Detroit.
Once a week in decent weather
he rows out to get a better
look at the opposite shore
as though Canada truly were
a foreign country. It isn't easy
what with the ore boats' lazy
crawl toward salt water, the launches
of tourists and cops, the lunchers
spread out on barges, docks, rafts,
waiting for the oiled clouds to lift
a moment and unveil the sun,
waiting for the fumes of exhaustion
to blow off in the poor gusts
of our making—collective breaths,
passing trucks, running dogs loath
to return to their chains.
On schedule he comes at noon
or not at all—his only free time—
so he can see with a painter's eye
the hulking shapes of warehouses define
themselves, the sad rusts and grays
take hold and shimmer a moment
in the blur of air until the stones
darken like wounds and become nothing.
He does this for our father
who parked each week exactly here
to stare at that distant shore
as though it were home, and then
passed quietly to a farther one.
He does this for me, who long ago
stopped seeing beneath the shadows
of concrete and burned brick towers
the flickering hints of life, the colors
we made of fresh earth and flowers

coming through the wet smells of houses
fallen in upon themselves. I suppose
he does this also so that somewhere
on the face of the black waters
he can turn, feathering one oar
slowly, to behold his own life
come into view brick by dark brick,
bending his back for all it's worth,
as the whole thing goes up in smoke.

THE SEVENTH SUMMER

How could I not know God had a son?
the biggest kid asked. I considered.
No one told me. Did I ever go to church?
Yes, but they spoke a language I didn't
actually understand. The three stared at me.
I could have answered that it was possible
God did not have a son and that this picture
over what was to be my bed was a fake—
for one thing it wasn't a photograph,
for another it looked like an ad from *Life*,
but I was already sorry I'd said, "Who
is he?" referring to the figure displayed
behind glass in a plain wooden frame.
What I truly wanted to know was why God
had let anyone do such a thing to his son,
nail his hands and feet to a huge wooden cross
from which he sagged in what appeared
to be less discomfort than I would have felt.
"The Jews done it," the biggest one said, as though
reading my mind. I felt a chill run through me,
sure that once more I was going to be blamed
for what I had not done or what I'd done
but done without meaning to do, but the boys
—the oldest was sixteen, over twice my age—left
me to myself, for it was early to bed for everyone.
I lay awhile in the silent dark of the farmhouse
wondering if it could be so, that God had
a son he had let die, and if this were so why
no one had told me so that I might understand
why life could be so puzzling for all of us.
Days passed before Lars, the fourteen year old,
told me that it was OK, this Jesus had died
so that all of us could be saved, in the end
things turned out for the best. That was Sunday,
after the boys had returned from church—
to which I did not go—, and before we walked
into town to swim in the big public place.

I remember best how sweet was the lake water
we swam in, how I could even swallow
little gulps of it and not feel ill and how large
the bodies around me were, Lars and Sven thrashing
after the girls in their dark wool suits, the girls
squealing with mock hurt when they would catch
them up in their pale arms, for though their faces
were deeply browned their bodies were ghostly.
Sven, Lars, and Thomas, three boys as big as men,
who let me climb to their secret room beside
the hay loft, where they smoked and spoke of women,
the laughter rushing out of their great throats,
the strange words I had never heard before coughed
out in sudden spasms, and such hopes uttered
as they moved about the room in a half-dance,
half-sword-fight, calling out the magic names
of the absent girls as they stroked their own bodies
at chest and crotch or rolled on the floor
in mock death agony. August in Michigan,
the world spinning around me, my mother gone
in the grief of final loss, from which one day
she would awaken in daylight, one year
before the wars in Ethiopia, Spain, and China
could give my growing up its particular name,
and yet I sat at their table that night, head bowed
in the grace I did not say, thankful for corn,
beans, and poisonous pork, and understood it all.

A NOTE ABOUT THE AUTHOR

Philip Levine was born in 1928 in Detroit and was for-
mally educated there, at the public schools and at Wayne
State University. After a succession of industrial jobs he
left the city for good and lived in various parts of the country before settling in Fresno, California, where he now
teaches. *The Names of the Lost* won the Lenore Marshall
Award for the best book of poetry published by an American in 1976. Three of his books have been nominated for
the National Book Critics Circle Award, and two of them,
Ashes and *7 Years from Somewhere*, have received it.
Ashes also received the American Book Award in 1980.
In 1987 he received the Ruth Lilly Poetry Prize "for distinguished poetic achievements," awarded by *Poetry* maga-
zine and The American Council for the Arts. His *New
Selected Poems* (which replaces the earlier *Selected Poems*
of 1984) is published simultaneously with *What Work Is*.

A NOTE ON THE TYPE

This book was set in Monticello, a Linotype revival of the original Roman No. 1 cut by Archibald Binny and cast in 1796 by the Philadelphia type foundry Binny & Ronaldson. The face was named Monticello in honor of its use in the monumental fifty-volume *Papers of Thomas Jefferson*, published by Princeton University Press. Monticello is a transitional type design, embodying certain features of Bulmer and Baskerville, but it is a distinguished face in its own right.

Composition by Heritage Printers, Inc., Charlotte, N. C.
Printed and bound by Halliday Lithographers,
West Hanover, Massachusetts
Designed by Harry Ford